Countries Around the World

Yemen

Jean F. Blashfield

www.raintreepublishers.co.uk
Visit our website to find out more information about Raintree books.

To order:
☎ Phone 0845 6044371
📄 Fax +44 (0) 1865 312263
💻 Email myorders@raintreepublishers.co.uk

Customers from outside the UK please telephone +44 1865 312262

Raintree is an imprint of Capstone Global Library Limited, a company incorporated in England and Wales having its registered office at 7 Pilgrim Street, London, EC4V 6LB – Registered company number: 6695582

Text © Capstone Global Library Limited 2012
First published in hardback in 2012
The moral rights of the proprietor have been asserted.

Edited by Louise Galpine
Designed by Richard Parker
Original illustrations © Capstone Global Library 2011
Illustrated by Oxford Designers and Illustrators
Picture research by Mica Brancic
Originated by Capstone Global Library Ltd.
Printed in China by CTPS

ISBN 978 1 406 22783 3 (hardback)
15 14 13 12 11
10 9 8 7 6 5 4 3 2 1

British Library Cataloguing in Publication Data
Blashfield, Jean F.
Yemen. --(Countries around the world)
953.3'053-dc22

Acknowledgements
We would like to thank the following for permission to reproduce photographs: Alamy pp. 9 (© Stefano Politi Markovina), 26 (© blickwinkel), 28 (© Michael Jenner), 30 (© Peter Adams Photography Ltd), 33 (© Michele Falzone); Corbis pp. 7 (© George Steinmetz), 12 (Xinhua Press/© Yin Ke), 13 (Reuters/© Aladin Abdel Naby), 15 (© Michel Gounot/Godong), 17 (Reuters/© Ahmed Jadallah), 22 (© Peter Adams), 23 (Reuters/© Khaled Abdullah), 25 (Reuters/© Ali Jarekji), 29 (Reuters/© Khaled Abdullah/X01740), 34 (© Barbara Davidson/Dallas Morning News), 37 (© George Steinmetz); Rex Features p. 31 (Startraks Photo); Shutterstock pp. 5, 8, 10 (© Vladimir Melnik), 18 (© kojik), 19 (© Arto Hakola), 20 (© Darklight), 35 (© Jovan Nikolic), 46 (© megastocker).

Cover photograph of Mahram Bilqis, Temple of the Sabaean Moon God Ilumquh, Yemen, reproduced with permission of Getty Images (The Image Bank/Daniele Pellegrini).

We would like to thank Peter Sluglett for his invaluable help in the preparation of this book.

Every effort has been made to contact copyright holders of any material reproduced in this book. Any omissions will be rectified in subsequent printings if notice is given to the publisher.

Contents

Some words are printed in bold, **like this**. You can find out what they mean by looking in the glossary.

Introducing Yemen

Yemen is an ancient land at the southern end of the Arabian **Peninsula**. Today, it is known as the Republic of Yemen, which, in Arabic, is *al-Jumhuriyah al-Yamaniyah*. The people themselves call it *al-Yaman*. This means "the south". Many people think it refers to being south of Mecca. Mecca is a city in Saudi Arabia, where Muhammad, founder of the religion of Islam, was born.

Fortunate Yemen

The ancient Romans called the land that became Yemen *Arabia Felix*, meaning "Fortunate Arabia". They thought the land was fortunate because people across the Mediterranean region were keen to buy the spices that grew there. It was also fortunate because its climate was less dry than other parts of the Arabian Peninsula. It had more mountains with generous amounts of rainfall and green valleys than any other place in that hot, desert region.

Yemen's location on the Red Sea is also fortunate. The narrow passageway, or **strait**, between Yemen and the African coast is called Bab al-Mandab. Throughout history much of the world's shipping travelled from the Mediterranean through the Red Sea to Bab al-Mandab, around Yemen, and into the Indian Ocean.

Today, Yemen is not so fortunate. It is now the poorest country in the Arab world. Keeping up with modern times is a challenge. But Yemen is a beautiful country, full of fascinating contrasts.

How to say...
When Yemenis greet each other they say "*as-salam alaykum*" (ah-suh-lahm uh-LAY-koom) which means "Hello" in Arabic.

Sana'a, Yemen's capital and largest city, was founded more than 2,500 years ago.

History: the making of a nation

Throughout history, invaders targeted Yemen because of its trade wealth. It came under the rule of a series of kingdoms. The first, more than 3,000 years ago, was the Minean kingdom. The second was the kingdom of Saba, also called Sheba, in about 900 BC. The third people to control the region were the Himyarites, who conquered Saba in about 25 BC.

Crossroads of trade

Among the goods that Yemenis sold to other countries were gold, frankincense, and myrrh. Gold is still mined in the region today. Frankincense and myrrh are made from the sap of trees that grow in Yemen. Ancient Egyptians used frankincense in making **incense**. They used myrrh in medicines and in turning bodies into mummies. Camels carried such goods along the Red Sea coast north to Egypt and then to Rome by sea.

Land routes were abandoned as the Romans learned to sail the Red Sea. Boats could travel faster and carry more goods than camels. Traders no longer had to pass through Yemen, and so the region's wealth gradually disappeared.

The Marib Dam

The people of Marib built one of the world's first dams in about 700 BC. It collected rainwater from the mountains. The water was used to **irrigate** huge gardens that fed thousands of residents. The Marib Dam collapsed in about AD 600. Probably one too many floods poured over the dam, weakening it. Many Yemenis became **nomads**, always on the move with their livestock, searching for water.

Visitors to Yemen often explore the ruins of the ancient city of Marib, which was the capital of Saba.

The coming of Islam

Other kingdoms came and went, but the biggest change in Yemen – one that still exists today – arrived from the north.

The beginning of Islam

In the city of Mecca, in Saudi Arabia, a boy named Muhammad was born about AD 570. As a young man he started receiving messages from God, whom he called Allah. Those messages were gathered in the book called the *Qur'an*. His ideas became the religion known as Islam. A **mosque**, or house of Islamic worship, was built as early as the 7th century in the Yemeni city of Sana'a.

Some mosques in Yemen were built in the 7th century. This one in Tarim was built around 100 years ago.

After Muhammad's death, his followers, called **Muslims**, divided. The group called **Sunnis** believed that the new leader should be elected from among those who were best qualified. The other group, the **Shi'is,** believed that the main leader must be a relative of Muhammad's or be appointed by God. Shi'i leaders, who were all **descendants** of Muhammad, were called imams.

For 1,000 years, starting in about AD 740, the leaders of Yemen were the imams from a Shi'i **sect** called the **Zaydis** (after Zayd, the fifth Shi'i imam) who had split off from the first Shi'is. About half of Yemenis, mostly those living in the highlands, still follow Zaydi Islam.

The Queen Arwa Mosque in Jibla contains the tomb of Queen Arwa.

QUEEN ARWA (1048–1138)

Queen Arwa al-Sulayhi was the wife of two different rulers of Saba, but she became the real leader of her people. After her second husband died in 1101, Arwa ruled on her own for another 37 years. She was well educated and studied science. She built roads and encouraged education and agriculture amongst her people.

North Yemen

The Zaydi imams ruled Yemen until 1517, when the **Ottoman** Turks invaded. They controlled it until 1630. The Ottomans returned to northern Yemen in the 1830s, and were eventually forced out after the end of World War I in 1918. (North Yemen is the triangular-shaped region north of Aden, near the Red Sea. Sana'a, today's capital, is located in the centre of North Yemen.)

The Zaydi imams took over again after the Ottomans left. The imams tried to shut out all foreigners. Several leaders were **assassinated**, and in 1962 **revolutionaries** took control. They called their new country the Yemen Arab Republic, or YAR.

Bab al Yemen, the main gate to the old city of Sana'a, is over 1,000 years old.

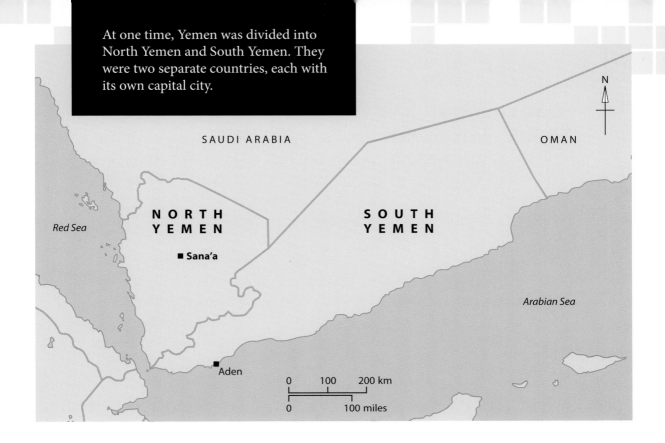

At one time, Yemen was divided into North Yemen and South Yemen. They were two separate countries, each with its own capital city.

South Yemen

The British **annexed** Aden in 1839, so they could break up the voyage to their colony in British India. They were able to control shipping through the Red Sea after the construction of the Suez Canal in 1869. This waterway allowed ships to travel from the Mediterranean Sea, through Egypt, and into the Red Sea. It meant ships from Europe did not have to travel around Africa to reach Asia. The British gradually occupied the whole of southern Yemen, with Aden as their capital. Their new **colony** became the Aden **Protectorate**.

In 1967, the British granted Aden its independence and left Yemen. The people of South Yemen formed the People's Democratic Republic of Yemen, or PDRY. The government of the PDRY decided to seek protection and money from the **Soviet Union**, which was under **communist** rule. Thousands of Yemenis who objected to communism **migrated** north to the Yemen Arab Republic.

One country

Several leaders of the YAR were assassinated. The military took over, and in 1978 Ali Abdullah Saleh (see panel on page 23), an army officer, became president of the YAR. He wanted the two Yemens to become one. The YAR, with 7 million people, and PDRY, with 2.3 million people, joined together on May 22, 1990. Saleh became president of the new Republic of Yemen, a position he still holds in 2010.

Even after the two Yemens joined to form one country, tensions between the two regions sometimes ran high. In 1994, these tensions erupted into civil war as southern leaders launched attacks against the north. Many southern leaders did not want to be part of a united Yemen. They wanted to re-establish their own nation, but the rebellion soon collapsed.

Yemeni men celebrating the unification of the two Yemens into the Republic of Yemen in 1990. The photo they are carrying is of President Saleh.

The damage to the USS *Cole* was extensive. The bomb destroyed a large portion of the port (left) side of the ship.

Terrorism

In recent times some people in Yemen have been supportive of **extremist** groups, especially **al-Qaeda**. The USS *Cole*, a US Navy destroyer, was refuelling in port at Aden on 12 October 2000. Men in a small boat deliberately crashed into the side of the ship. Seventeen American sailors were killed in the attack. *Al-Qaeda* claimed responsibility and several Yemenis were tried and found guilty.

Then, on 11 September 2001, *al-Qaeda* **terrorists** attacked the World Trade Center in New York City and the Pentagon in Washington DC, killing thousands. The Yemeni government decided it should help the United States in its fight against *al-Qaeda*. However, not all Yemenis agree with this.

Many attacks have been linked to Yemeni supporters of *al-Qaeda*. Yemen is now seen as a stronghold of *al-Qaeda*.

Regions and resources: great variety

Yemen lies on the highest part of the Arabian Peninsula, at the southwest corner. Hot, dry plains along the coasts lead inland to high **plateaus**, and many islands dot the sea. Much of Yemen is mountainous. It has two highland regions, one in the west and one in the centre of the country. Many peaks reach 3,000 metres (9,000 feet) above sea level. The land drops down at the coasts and towards the desert in the northeast. Long valleys, called **wadis**, collect water that runs from the mountains.

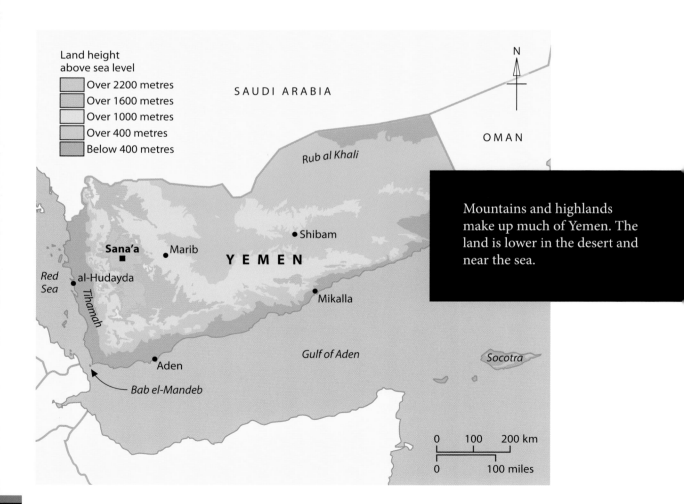

Land height above sea level

- Over 2200 metres
- Over 1600 metres
- Over 1000 metres
- Over 400 metres
- Below 400 metres

SAUDI ARABIA

OMAN

Rub al Khali

Shibam

Sana'a   Marib

YEMEN

Red Sea   al-Hudayda

Tihamah

Mikalla

Aden

Bab el-Mandeb

Gulf of Aden

Socotra

N

0   100   200 km

0   100 miles

Mountains and highlands make up much of Yemen. The land is lower in the desert and near the sea.

Most of Yemen's usable farmland is on **terraces** that were cut into the steep sides of mountains long ago.

The northern edge of Yemen is part of the Empty Quarter (*al-Rub' al-Khali*), a sand "sea" covering the Arabian Peninsula. Livestock eat the plants that hold soil together, meaning more soil is blown away and the desert expands. This **desertification** is swallowing up Yemen's usable land.

Water problems

Lack of fresh water is a problem in Yemen. The average Yemeni has only one-fiftieth the amount of drinkable water that the average person around the world has. Some businesses have taken advantage of Yemen's access to sea water to build factories that remove salt from seawater (**desalination**). Yemen's first desalination plant opened on the coast west of Sana'a in 2010.

Earth's forces

Earthquakes and volcanoes both feature in Yemen's recent past. A major earthquake in North Yemen in 1982 killed almost 3,000 people, about half of whom were children. In 2007, an underwater volcano formed a new island at the mouth of the Red Sea.

Agriculture

Most Yemenis work in agriculture, but there is little fertile land available. In the western highlands, the major crop is sorghum. Similar to corn, or maize, it grows where corn cannot. The eastern highlands produce wheat and barley.

Coffee originated in Africa but was brought to Yemen hundreds of years ago. It grows on terraces in the mountains between 900 and 2,100 metres (3,000 and 7,000 feet) above sea level. The coffee beans grow inside reddish fruits and then are roasted and ground. But today, much coffee-growing land has been replanted with *qat* (see below).

Daily life

Many Yemenis, especially men, gather in groups in the afternoon and evening to chat and laugh and chew *qat*. The leaves of the *qat* plant contain a chemical that makes people feel energized and alert. Some people worry that chewing *qat* can become an **addictive** habit.

Oil and gas

Oil, or petroleum, is the primary product of the Yemeni desert. The oil industry has brought rapid change to the region. Currently, the nation's economy is dependent on oil, but experts fear the oil will all be used up by 2017.

Many places where petroleum is found also produce **natural gas**. In the largest industrial project ever carried out in Yemen, natural gas is being **condensed** into liquid for shipment. The LNG, or liquefied natural gas, moves through a pipeline from Marib to Balhaf on the coast, where it is loaded into huge tanker ships. Yemen has enough LNG for at least 20 more years.

Small branches of the *qat*, or *khat*, plants are cut daily so that the leaves are fresh when chewed. They can also be dried and used to brew a tea.

Wildlife: birds, baboons, and dragon's blood

Yemen offers rare delights for nature lovers. The sky above is a flight path for birds migrating between Europe, Asia, and East Africa. During the spring and autumn, thousands of birds of prey cross Yemen. Inland, the large lake formed by the new Marib Dam is becoming a great area for bird watching.

The waters around Yemen are on the migration routes of six of the world's seven kinds of sea turtles. Those same six turtles are also on the world's **endangered** species lists. Many fish are disappearing due to changes in sea temperature caused by climate change. Still, skipjack and yellowfin tuna are thriving in Yemen's waters.

The Arabian leopard was named Yemen's national animal in 2008. It is estimated that fewer than 200 remain in the wild.

Colonies of baboons live throughout Yemen. Although the hamadryas baboon is one of Yemen's largest mammals, it is the world's smallest baboon. These baboons have long red faces and long fur. They live in groups of between 20 and 50 individuals.

The Hamadryas baboon lives near the Red Sea in both Yemen and East Africa.

The national park mountain

An isolated granite mountain called Jabal Bura is located west of Sana'a. The east side of the mountain has been terraced for agriculture, but the west side is completely wild. The rare valley forest found on its slopes is filled with endangered species. Rare acacia and myrrh trees grow there. Some of the species of plants and a few small animals are almost extinct. The area has been declared a national park.

One of the most unusual plants on Socotra is the dragon's blood tree, Yemen's national tree.

The island of Socotra

The large island of Socotra and three smaller nearby islands are all part of Yemen. Socotra lies about 380 kilometres (240 miles) from the mainland, closer to Somalia in Africa than to Yemen's mainland. It is about 130 kilometres (80 miles) long, with 1,500-metre (5,000-foot) mountains rising in the middle.

There are three towns on the island, all on the north side. The human population is about 50,000. They speak a form of Arabic called Soqotri. Some wealthier Yemenis have holiday homes on the island.

Unique species

Life has developed very differently on Socotra than on the Arabian Peninsula. There are about 700 species of plants and animals that are found only on the island. For example, the only cucumber plant that grows as a tree is found there. One of the island's most famous plants is the umbrella-shaped dragon's blood tree. It has red sap (the "dragon's blood") that once was used as medicine. It is still used in paint and varnish.

Several species of birds are also found nowhere else, including the Socotra sunbird and the Socotra warbler. They are endangered because cats on the island have turned wild, and they often kill the birds for food.

Around both Socotra and Zuqar Island in Bab al-Mandab are **coral reefs**. Holidaymakers put on snorkelling masks to explore the rocky reefs, getting a close-up view of the colourful fish and other sea creatures that live there. The reefs around Zuqar are part of Yemen's Marine National Park.

Infrastructure: how does Yemen work?

Sana'a, Yemen's largest city and capital, was founded about 2,500 years ago. Today, it has a population of almost two million. It is located in a valley at an elevation of 2,300 metres (7,546 feet), making it one of the highest capitals in the world. The central walled part of Sana'a is the Old City, and its Great Mosque is one of the oldest Islamic houses of worship in the world, built in about AD 630. The streets are narrow, so cars have little room to manoeuvre. The city outside the wall is more modern. Many wealthier Yemenis ride motorcycles to get around.

Sana'a was the capital of Yemen in ancient times, as it is today.

ALI ABDULLAH SALEH (1942–)

The military took charge of the Yemen Arab Republic in 1974. In 1978, Ali Abdullah Saleh, a lieutenant colonel in the Yemeni army, became president. In 1990, he succeeded in uniting the two parts of Yemen as the Republic of Yemen. He has been president ever since.

The national anthem

Created as the anthem of South Yemen, this song became the anthem of the new republic. Below is the English translation.

Repeat, O World, my song.
Echo it over and over again.
Remember, through my joy, each march.
Clothe him with the shining mantles
Of our festivals.

Repeat, O World, my song.
In faith and love am I part of mankind.
An Arab am I in all my life.
My heart beats in tune with Yemen.
No foreigner shall dominate over Yemen.

Daily life

When Yemeni people spend money, they use the Yemeni *rial*, or *riyal*. It is abbreviated to YR. There are 100 *fils* in a *rial*. Coins come in 5 and 10 *fils*, while notes are in 10 YR and higher.

Daily life

As with most cultures around the world, holidays play an important part in the lives of the Yemeni people. Some of the national holidays Yemenis celebrate are:

1 January: New Year's Day
26 February: Mouloud (Birth of the Prophet)
1 May: Labour Day
22 May: National Unity Day
26 September: Revolution Day
14 October: National Day
30 November: Independence Day

Representing the people

In Yemen, all citizens aged 18 and older can vote. The people elect a president and representatives. Yemen's legislature has two houses. The people elect the 301 members of the House of Representatives. The other house, called the Shura, has 111 members who are appointed by the president.

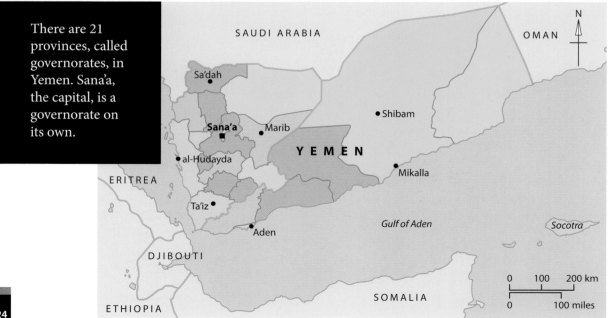

There are 21 provinces, called governorates, in Yemen. Sana'a, the capital, is a governorate on its own.

Governing Yemen

Yemen is divided into 21 different regions for administration. The regions are called **governorates**. The smallest is around Sana'a. The largest is Hadramawt, which stretches across the middle of the country.

Throughout large parts of Yemen, the most influential groups of people are **tribes**. Tribal leaders control groups of families called clans. They pay little attention to the current government as their tribes have existed far longer.

The economy

Yemen has the world's fourth fastest-growing population. It may reach 60 million by 2050. But Yemen does not have enough food, water, or jobs to support so many people.

The lack of jobs and the rate of population growth has become a major obstacle to progress in Yemen. The nation has an unemployment rate of almost 40 per cent.

These Yemeni women are showing that they voted in the presidential election.

Education

Since North Yemen and South Yemen united in 1990, public education has been free and required by law in Yemen. But there are many hidden fees and costs, such as uniforms, so poor families can rarely send their children to school.

Primary school lasts for six years and secondary for three more. The average girl attends school for only seven years. In 2008, the government started paying families of girls in poor rural areas to keep their daughters in school.

Poor people in parts of Yemen might live in huts like this one at Tihama.

YOUNG PEOPLE

Many Yemeni young people have to drop out of school to earn money for the family. Almost 25 per cent of children between 5 and 14 years work to earn money. *Al-Akhdam* originally came to Yemen as slaves. They have been in Yemen for hundreds of years but still live in poverty and face **discrimination**. An *Akhdam* father said, "I didn't go to school, nor did my father or grandfather. I need the children to help me collect empty cans and bottles to make a living."

Health care

Yemen's people receive little health care because of the nation's poverty. Yemen has only 3 doctors for every 10,000 people. This is compared to 21 per 10,000 in the United Kingdom and 27 per 10,000 people in the United States. Yemenis can expect to live to the age of 63, compared to 79 in the United Kingdom and 78 in the United States.

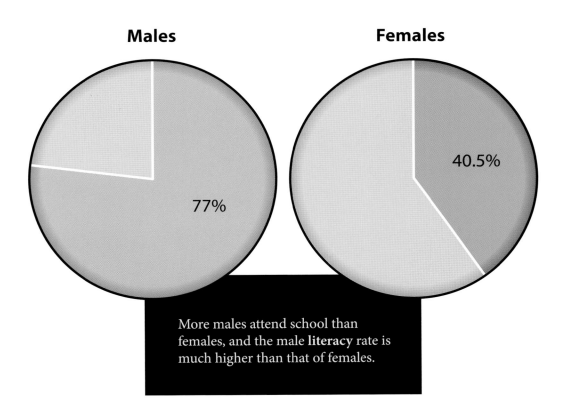

Males

77%

Females

40.5%

More males attend school than females, and the male **literacy** rate is much higher than that of females.

Daily life

One in ten of all Yemeni children born dies before the age of five. They are usually killed by diseases that are controlled elsewhere in the world by **vaccines**.

Culture: religion, art, and fun

Nearly all Yemenis are Muslim. Their religion is tied into everything they do and how they live. This is true whether they live in cities or as nomads in the desert.

Most Muslims pray five times every day. Many men go to the nearest mosque to pray. There are special sections in mosques for women, but they often pray at home. The official weekend is Thursday afternoon and Friday, with Friday as the day to worship in public.

Muslims usually identify themselves as either Sunni Muslims or Shi'i Muslims. Some rituals and practices differ between the two groups. But many others they share. For example, everyone who is at least 12 years old observes *Ramadan*. For one entire month, Muslims do not eat and drink between sunrise and sunset. The month reminds Muslims to be patient and modest, and to live a spiritual life.

Many boys go to religious school at their local mosque to learn to read the *Qur'an* in Arabic.

Refugee camps host thousands of Somali Muslim families who have escaped war at home and fled to safety in Yemen.

Other religions

Only a few hundred Jews live in Yemen today. When the Jewish state of Israel was founded in 1948, many Jews living in the Middle East were forced to move there. Almost 50,000 Yemeni Jews went to Israel.

Today there are more Christians than Jews in Yemen. In 2010, the number was estimated at about 9,000. Most Christian churches are in Aden, which was British territory until 1967.

How to say...

When Muslims talk about a future event, they add, *"Insha'Allah"* (insh-uh-LAH), which means "God willing".

Women and girls

In Yemen, women can drive cars, vote, own property, and get divorced. But still, they often have little control over their lives. Traditionally, parents arrange a marriage for their daughters, often at a very young age and to men they may never have met.

Women in rural areas work constantly. They fetch water, collect wood, prepare food, tend the fields, care for children, and look after grazing animals. They usually do all this dressed in long robes. Few of them can read and write.

A woman wearing a *sharshaf* walks in a bazaar in Sana'a.

In the privacy of their own homes, women may wear whatever they choose. But when a woman goes out in public, she is most likely to hide her clothing under a *sharshaf*, a robe that fully covers her. The part on the head is called the *hijab*, and the veil covering the face is called the *niqab*. Only a narrow slit is left for the woman's eyes to see where she is going. Some women, especially professional women or those tending the fields, do not wear the robe or veil, but all women cover their hair.

Shada Nasser (right) and Nujood Ali attend the Glamour Women of the Year awards in 2008. Nasser helped Ali divorce her abusive, much-older husband.

SHADA NASSER (1964–)

Born in Aden in 1964 but raised in Prague, in what is now the Czech Republic, Shada Nasser became a lawyer. In 1989, she returned to Yemen and was the only female lawyer in the capital city. She concentrated on cases involving human rights. When 10-year-old Nujood Ali wanted to divorce her brutal, 30-year-old husband, Nasser took on the case. In 2008, she succeeded in making Nujood the youngest divorced woman in the world.

Housing

Yemeni cities, especially Sana'a, have been described as looking like iced gingerbread. The houses are usually tall and made of brownish stone decorated with a lighter coloured plaster (see picture on page 5). Men and women live on different floors of the multi-storey houses. They even have separate entrances. Little furniture is used. Mattresses are moved out at night for sleeping and tucked away during the day.

In a tradition dating back before the coming of Islam, one window in every room has geometric shapes of stained glass. At night, the cities become colourful as light shines through these windows.

The arts

One of the most popular forms of Yemeni literature is the *zamil*, a poem usually made up on the spot, at weddings or political gatherings. Each consists of only two lines.

Islam forbids showing people in religious art. Most art in Yemen, therefore, consists of beautiful decorations on mosques. Sometimes the decorations are elaborate writings showing verses from the *Qur'an*.

The human voice is the main instrument in traditional Yemeni music. Yemeni songs are often based on poetry.

ABDULLAH AL-BARADOUNI
(1929-1999)

Yemen's most prominent writer in recent years has been Abdullah al-Baradouni. He wrote many books of poetry as well as political titles. He was blinded by disease as a small child, but he went on to become a teacher of Arabic literature.

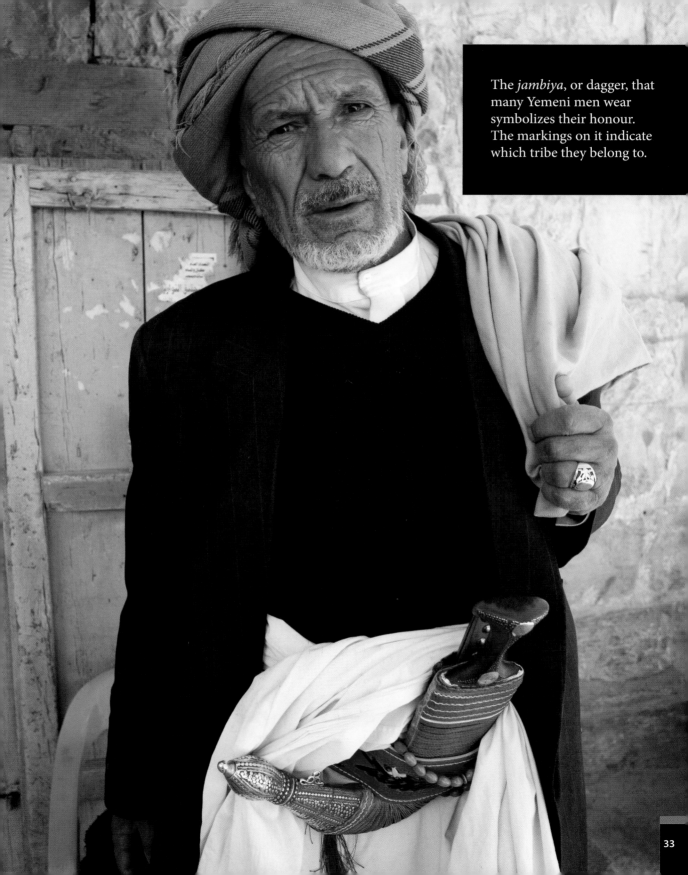

The *jambiya*, or dagger, that many Yemeni men wear symbolizes their honour. The markings on it indicate which tribe they belong to.

Sports

Among both children and adults, the most popular sport in Yemen is football. The Yemeni team competes in a tournament called the Arabian Gulf Cup. Yemen has never won, but it hosted the event in 2010.

Women often play basketball, table tennis, volleyball, and take part in gymnastics. Because they get little support from families or government, women find it hard to make sports anything more than a hobby. This attitude may change as more people watch international sports on television. They have a role model in Yemeni-born Isra Gisgrah. She was raised in Canada and became a world champion female boxer.

Children play football wherever they can find room.

Food

In most homes, the main meal of the day is at noon. The national dish, *saltah*, is often served. It is a soupy combination of meat, rice, beans, and sometimes eggs. It is eaten with flatbread. Although Yemen grows excellent coffee, most people drink tea.

Bulgar wheat and honey dessert recipe

Ask an adult to help you cook this tasty dessert.

Ingredients

- 180 grams bulgar wheat, rinsed
- ½ teaspoon salt
- 1 litre water
- 1 teaspoon cinnamon
- ¼ teaspoon crushed cloves
- 175 grams honey

Instructions

Place the bulgar wheat, salt, and water in a saucepan, and then bring it to the boil. Put the lid on the pot, and turn the heat down to low. Simmer for 40 minutes or until the wheat is well-cooked. If all the water boils out, add more. Stir in the remaining ingredients. Serve the dessert hot.

Bulgar wheat, can be sweetened with honey and eaten as a dessert.

Yemen today

Long isolated, Yemen is rapidly entering the 21st century. Though few Yemenis have had telephones in the past, mobile phones are becoming common. Children are learning to use computers and the Internet in school. In 2010, a huge outdoor TV screen was set up in Sana'a's stadium so people could watch the World Cup football matches from South Africa. For many Yemenis, that was their first experience of watching television.

How to say...

When Yemenis part ways, they say, "*Ma'a salama*" (MAH sal-ah-mah) which means "Goodbye" in Arabic.

The future

Yemen's future is uncertain. In the north, Zaydi Shi'is rebelled when the Sunni government seemed to ignore them. In the south, many citizens want to separate again from the north. They think the oil from their lands is being stolen by the government.

The presence of *al-Qaeda* in Yemen causes problems; Yemeni soldiers are often killed in bomb attacks on police stations. Some Yemenis work with *al-Qaeda* because they need jobs. But the people of Yemen are proud and independent.

Yemen is beautiful and fascinating, but little is done to encourage tourism. Some people from other countries fear that they will be kidnapped and held for ransom by rural tribespeople. The kidnappers usually don't demand money. Instead, they want to force the government to do work that is needed, such as building bridges or improving the electricity supply.

Many Yemenis are concerned that both the government and *al-Qaeda* are working against them. They continue to hold out hope for a better future.

Shibam, the historic city of high-rise mud buildings, draws tourists to the eastern part of Yemen.

Fact file

Official Name: Republic of Yemen

Capital: Sana'a

Official language: Arabic

State religion: Muslim

Population: 23,495,361 (2010 estimated)

Largest cities: Sana'a, al-Hudaydah,Ta'izz, Aden

Type of government: Republic

Divisions: 21 governorates

Bordering countries: Oman, Saudi Arabia

Area: 527,968 square kilometres (203,849 square miles)

Coastline: 1,906 kilometres (1,184 miles)

Major rivers: None; longest *wadi*, or dry river valley, is Wadi Hadramawt, 240 kilometres (149 miles) long

Highest point: Jabal al- Nabi Shu'ayb, 3,660 metres (12,028 feet) above sea level

Lowest point: Arabian Sea, sea level

Average annual rainfall: 51 to 91 centimetres (20 to 36 inches)

Resources: oil, natural gas, fish, marble

Main imports:	Food, machinery, chemicals
Main exports:	oil, LNG (liquefied natural gas), coffee, dried fish
Major trading partners:	United Arab Emirates, China, Thailand
Currency:	Yemeni *rials* (abbreviated YR)
Life expectancy:	63 years
Literacy rate:	49 per cent (male: 77 per cent, female: 40.5 per cent)
Poverty rate:	45 per cent
National anthem:	"United Republic", words by Abdallah Abdulwahab, nomen and music by Ayoob Tarish Absey
Prominent Yemenis:	Arwa, queen of Saba (1048–1138)
	Ayoob Tarish Absey, musician and composer of national anthem (1942–)
	Abdullah al-Baradouni, poet (1929–1999)
	Isra Gisgrah, five-time female world champion boxer (1971–)
	Shada Nasser, human rights lawyer (1964–)
	Ali Abdallah Saleh, president (1942–)

Timeline

BC

ca. 900	The kingdom of Saba, or Sheba, is founded.
ca. 700	The Marib Dam, one of world's earliest dams, is built.
ca. 25	The Himyarite Kingdom conquers Saba.

AD

ca. 600	The Marib Dam collapses.
ca. 740	Zaydi Shi'i imams rule Yemen.
1101	Queen Arwa becomes ruler of Saba.
1517	Ottoman Turks invade Yemen and control it for about 100 years.
1830s	Ottomans return to northern Yemen .
1839	British forces take over Aden.
1869	The Suez Canal connecting the Red Sea with the Mediterranean Sea opens; Aden becomes an important refuelling stop for shipping.
1918	The Ottomans are forced out of northern Yemen.
1937	The British establish the Aden Protectorate.
1962	The military takes control of North Yemen and turns it into the Yemen Arab Republic.
1967	The British give up Aden; the city becomes capital of the People's Democratic Republic of South Yemen.

1972   Border fighting breaks out between the north and the south.

1978   Ali Abdullah Saleh becomes president of the Yemen
        Arab Republic.

1982   An earthquake in North Yemen kills 3,000 people.

1990   The Yemen Arab Republic and the People's Democratic Republic
        of Yemen join to form the Republic of Yemen.

1994   A war breaks out between southern and northern Yemen.

2000   The USS *Cole* is attacked by *al-Qaeda* terrorists in Aden Harbour;
        17 American sailors die.

2001   Terrorists attack the World Trade Center in New York City and the
        Pentagon in Washington, DC; Saleh tells the United States that
        Yemen is its partner in fighting terrorism.

2010   Yemen remains a stronghold of *al-Qaeda*.

Glossary

AD short for *Anno Domini*, which is Latin for "in the year of our Lord". When this appears before a date, it refers to the time after the Christian religion began.

addictive habit forming

al-Qaeda network of terrorists who were responsible for the 2001 attack on the World Trade Center in New York City and the Pentagon in Washington, DC

annex add to one's own territory

assassinate murder an important person such as the leader of a country

BC means "before Christ". When this appears after a date it refers to the number of years before the Christian religion began. BC dates are always counted backwards.

colony community settled in a new land but with ties to another government

communist belonging to a system in which all property and goods are owned by everyone and controlled by the government

condense to change from gas to liquid

coral reef colourful rocky structure in warm seas formed from the skeletons of animals called coral polyps

desalination removal of salt from sea water

descendant offspring of an earlier group

desertification process of becoming desert

discrimination unequal treatment based on race, gender, religion, or other factors

endangered at some risk of dying out

extremist someone who behaves in an unreasonable way

governorate administrative division of a country headed by a governing leader

incense material that gives off a sweet-smelling smoke when burned

irrigate water crops

literacy ability to read and write

migrate travel to another location, usually covering a long distance

mosque building where Muslims worship

Muslim person who follows the religion of Islam

natural gas gas that can be ignited and burned; usually found under ground near petroleum

nomad someone who travels from place to place rather than settling down

Ottoman Turkish, during the period from the 14th to the 20th century when the Ottoman Empire controlled the Middle East

peninsula land surrounded by water on three sides

plateau raised flat area of land

protectorate small country ruled by a larger one

revolutionary someone who wants to overthrow the government

sect religious group consisting of members with similar beliefs

Shi'i follower of the branch of Islam that believes that only Muhammad's family and descendants have spiritual authority over Muslims

Soviet Union communist country that stretched from eastern Europe across Asia. It broke apart into several smaller countries in 1991.

strait narrow waterway connecting two larger bodies of water

Sunni follower of the branch of Islam that believes that anyone capable of leading Muslims can have authority

terrace horizontal ridge made in a hillside that helps preserve soil and moisture so that crops can be grown

terrorist person who uses violence to try to force change

tribe collection of families who are linked by their history and culture

vaccine medicine, usually given in an injection, that prevents someone from getting a specific disease

wadi dry river valley that may fill during heavy rains

Zaydi branch of Shi'ism that controlled North Yemen for many years. Almost half of the Yemenis in the north belong to Zaydi tribes.

Find out more

Books

An Illustrated Atlas of Europe (Continents in Close-up), Malcolm Porter (Cherrytree Books, 2007)

I Am Nujood, Age 10 and Divorced, Nujood Ali (Three Rivers Press, 2010)

Stories from Islam (Stories From Faiths), Rohail Aslam (Heinemann Library, 2008)

The Islamic Empires (Time Travel Guides), Anna Claybourne, John Haywood, Richard Spilsbury (Raintree, 2008)

Islam (World Faiths), Trevor Barnes (Kingfisher Books, 2005)

Websites

www.yementourism.com
Find details and photos of places to visit in Yemen on this website.

www.yementimes.com
A weekly newspaper in English bringing readers feature stories and information on current events in Yemen.

www.al-bab.com
Calling itself an "open door to the Arab world", this site pulls together links from many different sources.

https://www.cia.gov/library/publications/the-world-factbook/geos/ym.html
Visit this website for lots of facts and figures about Yemen.

www.lonelyplanet/yemen.com
Learn more about the country from a tourist's point of view.

Places to visit

Dar al-Hajar

Dar al-Hajar, or Rock Palace, is a palace built a few miles from Sana'a in Wadi Dhahr.

UNESCO World Heritage Sites in Yemen (http://whc.unesco.org/en/statesparties/ye):
Sana'a

Sana'a, or The Old City, is located in the governorate of Sana'a.

Shibam

Located in the governorate of Hadramout, Shibam is a 16th-century vertical city built of mud.

Zabid

The historic town of Zabid, located in the governorate of al-Hudayda, is the site of an early Islamic university and was capital of Yemen from the 13th to 15th centuries.

Socotra Archipelago

These islands contain distinct plant and animal life because of their isolated location.

Topic tools

You can use these topic tools for your school projects. Trace the map onto a sheet of paper, using the thick black outline to guide you.

The flag of the Republic of Yemen shows its unity with other Arab countries. Egypt, Syria, Iraq, and other Arab nations use the same three stripes of red, white, and black. The red represents the blood shed in the fight for freedom, the white symbolizes hope for the future, and the black represents the dark past that lies behind it. Copy the flag design and then colour in your picture. Make sure you use the right colours!

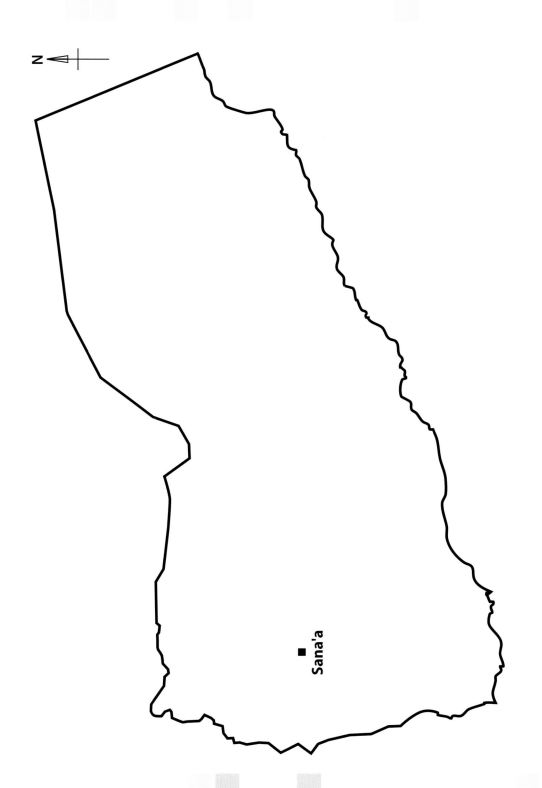

N

Sana'a

Index

Titles in the series

Afghanistan	978 1 406 22778 9
Brazil	978 1 406 22785 7
Chile	978 1 406 22786 4
Costa Rica	978 1 406 22787 1
Cuba	978 1 406 22788 8
Czech Republic	978 1 406 22792 5
England	978 1 406 22799 4
Estonia	978 1 406 22793 2
France	978 1 406 22800 7
Germany	978 1 406 22801 4
Haiti	978 1 406 22789 5
Hungary	978 1 406 22794 9
India	978 1 406 22779 6
Iran	978 1 406 22780 2
Iraq	978 1 406 22781 9
Italy	978 1 406 22802 1
Latvia	978 1 406 22795 6
Lithuania	978 1 406 22796 3
Mexico	978 1 406 22790 1
Pakistan	978 1 406 22782 6
Poland	978 1 406 22797 0
Scotland	978 1 406 22803 8
Wales	978 1 406 22804 5
Yemen	978 1 406 22783 3